Book One - Financial Literacy Basics - SFL

Life and Debt

Workbook Q&A

A companion workbook to *Good Debt, Bad Debt* by Jon Hanson

Created to support **Stewardship for Life**,
a 501(c)(3) For Impact Public Charity
SFLToday.org

written by: Jon Hanson
editor: Tiffany Koenig
cartoons: Patty Kadel

"Life is great when you spend less than you make!"
SFLToday.org

"Emotional spending is the 'drunk driving' of financial stewardship."
Jon Hanson, March 5, 2014

Whether you have received this workbook digitally or in old-school paper book form, as part of the SFL home study course or from Amazon.com, *I want to personally thank you for supporting Stewardship for Life.*

ISBN-13:
978-0692025291 (SFLToday.org)

ISBN-10:
0692025294

Published by Stewardship for Life | SFLToday.org | A For-Impact Organization

If you have a copy of this material that you know has not been paid for (and that actually bothers you) please consider going to SFLToday.org and make a general donation. That way you won't have to keep looking over your shoulder for the Karma Bus.

Table of Contents

Preface: It's about time *and* money!

Understanding financial literacy without sensible application will not make you wealthy; but ignoring the lessons of this program will keep you poor. As with all educational material, you should rely on common sense when evaluating this or any program. In matters of taxes, legal, real estate, securities, financial planning, or advice it is recommended you seek competent and appropriate counsel.

My goal is that all SFL materials, web classes, and live seminars will help supporters and participants make better life decisions. I am personally asking you for a 10 year commitment to sane rational financial stewardship! Increasing your income while controlling expenses may speed your process to financial sustainability. This program requires *work* and *planning*. Our products challenge you to embrace hard truths; truths a majority of Americans currently ignore. I will always value successful participants and supporters over increased product sales. There are no quick cures for years of poor stewardship. **The actual cure requires me to speak straight forward and plainly to you (tough love). No hype. Do you understand? 10 years, or more.**

Thank you again for supporting Stewardship for Life's mission: **To help alleviate poverty, whether generational, situational, or self-inflicted.** Only when the basic needs are covered can you genuinely live a life of purpose, find work you love, and matter in your life and others'.

2014

Jim Rohn used to say, "If you knew better, you'd do better." Beyond knowing, there is the more difficult element…doing!

In the song bridge of "Credit Card Junkie" (Hanson, 2009) included in the optional audio portion of this home study guide, the words are: *"I love the high I get from spending, even though I know it's crazy / I want what I want and I want it now / It'll take more than 12 steps to save me!"*

Deep down, most of us instinctively know what to do. The financial stewardship *game* (more than 80 percent, perhaps) is played in your mind. It is very much a game, and because of the money, it is a professional game. In your personal home version, you are paid (rewarded) if you play well and penalized if you play poorly (or don't play).

Seemingly, most of what successful folks *do* to be successful is boring at best—yet absolutely essential. Throughout *Good Debt, Bad Debt* I use humor, cartoons, bite-sized lessons, and sarcasm to show us human beings being human.

Just as rich foods are pleasurable, so too is promiscuous spending. The part of life where you match up your words with your actions is the most troubling for many people (assuming you want a secure future).

Certainly excuses are very useful: they allow you to skip like a flat rock across the river of common sense, analysis, and real-life testing. If you are like me, the majority of your personal stewardship life will be dealing with *your* emotions and reasons for spending. We can have excuses, or we can have results. Eric Hoffer's admonition "A man with an excuse is set for life," (Hoffer, 1966) is illustrative here.

Right-sizing your spending, eliminating debt, and saving for prolonged senior moments (retirement) may be as difficult as sustained weight loss, quitting nicotine, or using *The Browns* and *Super Bowl* in a sober sentence. As to food, you may be physically addicted to caffeine, carbs, or chocolate, but it is the obsessive thoughts of food—pleasurable memories—that lead us to seek the next "fix." (Volek & Phinney, 2011).

Is there is a physical aspect to spending also? I think there is. It may be short, hollow, and ultimately empty, but it's there. Neuroscientist David J. Linden of John Hopkins University School of Medicine, in *The Compass of Pleasure*, discloses how chocolate, fatty foods, sex, and gambling, among other things, manipulate our pleasure senses contained within the medial forebrain pleasure circuit, leading to ever-increasing desires or cravings with a lessening of satisfaction each time. In the end, most addicts end up with a blunted ability to sense (profit from or enjoy) the pleasure they seek from their vice. They expect more but ultimately seem to get less (Linden, 2012).

Linden also discusses gambling, which is exactly what we are doing with our future (and our families) when we operate to satiate pleasures versus implementation of a well thought-out plan for our financial lives. Brain scan research has shown gamblers receive nearly as much pleasure from "almost" winning as actually winning. Perhaps profligate spending, for some, is driven by a similar principle.

Is there a way to move financial discernment to a source of pleasure? I don't know. I do know the end results of good stewardship can be pleasurable and satisfying. It seems the greater the distance between reward and pleasure, the harder it is to sustain the path to attainment. For example, cheesecake (insert your own vice) has a pretty quick payoff of pleasure, while adding $50 a week to your IRA is part of a long, slow process.

It may be a worthy area of study to pursue, a few researchers (Oaten & Cheng, 2006) have studied long-term benefits of developing sensible habits over time. I personally know a handful of people who naturally choose delayed gratification. (Linden might say their pleasure sensors are wired or set differently.) I'd like to design a project comparing an income segment of the population to folks that are coached to learn sensible long-term habits—the second key element I hinted at earlier.

Why do *some* people overspend and not provide for their future, in face of overwhelming evidence of the severe consequences that will befall them? I suspect humans (at least my kind) have a most sophisticated rationalization and excuse-making mechanism that can override common sense, rational thought, and even simple math. Many of us embrace the unearned optimism of an unknown future.

What if right-sizing your *spending-to-income ratio* could become as high a priority as Twinkies to Honey Boo Boo's mom? What if the financial discernment gene, desire, or *even craving* could be bred into politicians? I know, I went too far. It would be easier to make hyenas vegan.

Positive Thinking Isn't Enough

Most inspirational prosperity gurus, preachers, teachers, and infomercial mavens do a disservice to their clients by doing only a "rolling stop" on the actual work and discipline of training the good habits it takes to operate a successful financial life (or life at all). They do have one thing right: *thinking* is the beginning of making any of your wishes come true. But please don't believe it takes *only* thinking, chanting, or vibrating at the right frequency to be successful. Within the multitude of things these prosperity preachers claim to "manifest" into their lives, empirical scientific journals never seem to be among them. At some point real success (as opposed to talk only) will require deliberate and thoughtful action.

Beyond the point where the guru signs off with his followers left in the warm glow of envisioning their futures, we will find the real work of becoming successful. It is well to begin with the end in mind (Covey, 1989) but equally important to **visualize the process** it will take to get to said end, and how and when such steps will happen (Keller & Papason, 2011). If you will allow me a bit of parody poetry that came to me while listening to *The One Thing* audio book and editing this introduction at my Starbucks 9404 office (I have locations all over the world). With apologies to Louisa Mae Alcott:

Habit

I slept, and dreamed that life was thought
I woke, and found life as my habits wrought.
Do dreams foreshadow or do they lie?
Days of toil, I have pursued courageously.
Still distant dreams will they ever be?
Suddenly I see! 'Tis my habits that have made me.

—Jon Hanson, March 7, 2014, well caffeinated during my Saturday morning time block.

The Daily Practice

Along with training the habits that will ultimately decide or derail your success, there has to be a realistic time commitment. **Overnight *successes* are often at the end of ten year *stretches*.** Perhaps the contrived rhyme will help you remember that line! Less poetically, in *Outliers* (Gladwell, 2008) we read that it takes 10,000 hours of work to achieve mastery in a given area. Understand, please, this means steady progress leading toward mastery; not 10,000 hours of doing it wrong. Gladwell's story of how the Beatles actually became the Beatles playing in Hamburg, Germany, 8 to 10 hours a night is worth the price of the book.

Most Everything Good Happens in the First Six Feet

So yes, read *Think and Grow Rich*, but then also read (or listen to) *The One Thing* by Gary Keller and Jay Papason (2012), a decidedly more practical guide to success. Many programs *like* to keep you mentally at the 30,000-foot view, or the 10,000-foot view (exciting, isn't it?). Vision statements and grandiose mission statements are the easy part; they fly high above actual doing. It's fun to take a ride-along with the "Air Force" to survey the land and perhaps drop a few bombs. As I have discussed with my kids, the hard fact is, most results in life are achieved in the first six feet of the atmosphere. Like it or not, much of life involves hand-to-hand combat (mostly with yourself). Dealing with your own success and cleaning up debt is a ground war.

Are there "life hacks" or shortcuts to competency? Certainly! You may advance toward mastery quicker by studying and developing a clear philosophy of financial literacy and how it ebbs and flows into most every area of your life. Additionally, be certain to model someone you admire. Perhaps a friend or relative who is a squared-away soldier in the area of personal finances could be a model. Think in ten-year time blocks, have the end in mind, and then create step goals and objectives with daily actions that lead you to where you wish to be. Success is a process not a leap to mastery.

No! No! I said you have to have a PURPOSE!

The Picture of Good Stewardship

When my wife and I traveled to Kauai, Hawaii, in 2013, I was surprised to learn that a pineapple takes three years to grow. I like pineapple, but seriously, three years? We humans are impatient. **How long is reasonable to develop a fully formed *self-sustaining human being?*** More than a pineapple, certainly. My observation is 10 or 20 years of working life to fully develop; assuming sane and rational habits are engaged. I have actual models (friends) who, for many years, have followed the practices I came to, and am still learning, late in life. Whether growing pineapples or little humans there are best practices (processes) that if followed, net excellent results.

Back to the picture. What does a well-lived life of financial literacy look like? To answer the question, my handful of exemplars and their partners can generally move freely about the world anytime they want to—without incurring debt or depleting capital. This fact alone sets them apart from 97 percent of the population.

What is different about them than the less financially astute? They made work, their first twenty years after school, a stage of life, not their life. Now they are no longer subject to loss of freedom from debt or a J-O-B, or a soul-sucking business they really don't love (I am amazed at the number of people who work for themselves and hate their boss). Of course, they have funds for material pleasures, but the real wealth they have is peace of mind.

Once our exemplars reached the point where their savings and investment income took care of all their needs, they became "fire proof" as the late Jack Miller used to say. When you are fire proof, and no one can threaten your existence with loss of income, your worldview can change a great deal. The austere practices (Smart Daily Choices) that these exemplars employed over the past 30 years or more have allowed them freedom to work or not work if they choose.

In the conclusion to *Good Debt, Bad Debt,* I quote Longfellow: "Most people would succeed in small things if they were not troubled with great ambitions." Many of us are good at making the "right" proclamations but fail in the small "smart" daily decisions that are the foundation of a life of financial success.

> ***Exemplar*** means an admired person or thing that deserves to be copied. The finest example available, my friends Dan and Tracy, are to financial stewardship as Dale Earnhardt was to NASCAR.

The Practice of Good Stewardship

- People often confuse strategy (what-how, or *What's really going on here?*) with their goals (outcome). According to strategy expert Richard Rumelt's "kernel" of good strategy theory (Rumelt, 2011), the kernel of all good strategy has these three critical elements (below are quick partial examples):

    a) **An accurate diagnosis**. "I'm forty and could live 50 to 60 more years. My wants and desires far exceed my present income. If I cannot right-size my outgo to my income, I will suffer greatly later, especially if I use debt for said desires."
    b) **Guiding principles**. List how you will handle emotional spending opportunities, when you will use debt, debt elimination if applicable, delayed gratification, daily coherent action, and application of the Burn Rate principle. A rational plan for houses, spouses, and cars, oh my!
    c) **Day-to-day plan of operation to implement strategy**. "I will track and tabulate in writing, on a smart phone, or on computer all spending for six months or a year, or until I am operating well within an acceptable burn rate."

- Responsive reading (congregation's part is in **bold**): So-called good debt has to do with **an outcome or a result**. Therefore, good debt means borrowing only in the **rare** instance that you can **create a situation that produces a return in excess of the *cost and risk* of using the debt**. Good debt is an **outcome**, not a reflection (or warm fuzzy feeling) of what the debt is used for or how it is borrowed. Debt for education, business, and real estate is **not always good debt**! Pass it on, go forth, and spend no more (than necessary). Amen.
- Build a list of guiding principles or core beliefs that you can come back to when you get lost or off track.
- Understand that bad debt is a claim on your future earnings and does not pay for anything, but merely defers the payment. Don't suffer from the Kristofferson-Joplin effect, where you: "Trade all your tomorrows for one single yesterday…"
- Start where you are. If you need remedial, embrace remedial. Embracing good stewardship will be remedial for many of us. Remember: you can't *should have done* something, but you can *do something* NOW. Review "Parable of the Marbles" (p. 71 in 2007 *Good Debt, Bad Debt*)
- From an early age, resolve to lay aside a portion of all you earn. If you missed this appointment with destiny, as many of us have, take the next best time: NOW.
- Don't sweat the math! If you cannot save 10 percent at first, save 1, 3, 5, 7, 8, 9 percent, etc. The idea is to begin. Even a small win is a beginning. **Fall/fail forward.**

- Be able to state a reason for your new optimism if questioned. "Because I read *Good Debt, Bad Debt*," though a lovely start, is not enough.
    a) Avoid "happy hope" as Jim Rohn says, "The man is 40 and broke and he's ha--appy!?[the WTH? is implied]" With no plan, you fit Mr. Rohn's description of "happy hope" or what I refer to as "optimistic taffy," a product many chew to distract from reality (things will work out right?). I promise it is only possible to gain self-esteem through YOUR education, effort, and enterprise. The "self" in self-esteem should be a clue about its nexus.
    b) Embrace your Inner Drill Sergeant: **"You may be as unique as a snowflake, but the world has a lot of broke snowflakes.** Is that what you want? You may revel in your uniqueness or adapt the best from excellent models. Are you still with me? I'm being mean right now, aren't I?
    c) Try something like this: "I am reducing my debt by 20 percent this year and increasing my savings from 0 to 2, then 3, then 5 percent this year. My plan eliminates all of my debt in 84 months. I know I am in a hole, and have stopped digging (I am smart enough to know I can't borrow more in this 84 months). Once I have completed my Debt Warfare plan, it will allow me to redirect my former debt payments to my 'fireproof fund.' I am working to educate myself to be able to give more value to my employer or my customers, **thereby *increasing the value I bring to the market and therefore what I earn.*"**
    d) Read and understand the **LERI** concept on p. 58 *Good Debt, Bad Debt* (2007 edition). Review Chapter 6 "What if You Live?" on p. 110.
- If you absolutely cannot cut spending by 1, 2, or 3 percent even, you should consider a run for congress. That is the plan they follow (they can't even dial back the automatic increases). A senate seat is a million-dollar contract ($174,000 x 6 years) plus benefits (and a staff).
- Goals and cool mission statements are fine things, but make sure they have an actionable daily plan. We grow wealthy or broke by our Daily Choices (DC): either Smart Daily Choices (SDC) or Dumb Daily Choices (DDC). Read *The Compound Effect* (Hardy, 2010). Once good habits are installed, I like to think of them collectively as The Daily Practice (TDP).
- Trust in your ability to learn as you go. I have titled my 2014 prevailing attitude as **Iterative Innovation**—that is, I want to learn from learning. "Iterative" because I am slowly improving on my existing knowledge and innovative, because I seek to link the learning or delivery methods for *Stewardship for Life* in new ways and in the most cost-effective way I can achieve. I am committed to lifelong learning. The spreading of the Core4 areas (see FAQs at SFLToday.org) that make up SFL's educational message may take the form of books, online courses, classroom/seminars, audio or video (or whatever is next—Satellite to Google Glass?).

The Promise of Good Stewardship

> "The pith of all the world's wisdom on *money getting* is condensed into a few proverbs. To work hard, to improve small opportunities, to economize, to avoid debt, are the general rules in which is summed up the hoarded experience of centuries, and the most sagacious writers have added little to them." William Matthews, in *Getting On in the World* (Matthews, 1878).

My promise: **If you will do for ten years what most people will never do, you will be *on your way* or *able to* do whatever you want to do for the remainder of your life.** The timeframe may be longer if you are besot with debt or if you presently have the pathology of Income Deficit Syndrome (IDS):

1. **High rent** (exceeds 30 percent of income)
2. **Low skills** (begets low earnings)
3. **Rising hopelessness** (survival mode).

With IDS, staying above water consumes so much time that it's hard to discover a way out. This is often the legacy of generational poverty (Payne, 2005). Without proper training (of habits) the affected are no better off doubling their income. Any help given to low- to moderate-income individuals, in my view, should build and sustain self-reliance, not become an opportunity for more consumer debt, increasing dependency, or profligate spending.

I Know, You're Different, Snowflake…

It doesn't matter if you're 20 or 60. If you're suffering from generational or situational poverty, *or self-inflicted poverty* (your own bad money management), the cure is the same: spend less than you make to progress forward financially. For low-income individuals in the second quintile of earners, averaging $27,500 per year (Income Statistics, 2014) the hard part is downshifting enough while surviving, and learning to increase income.

Of course, it's far more difficult for a single mother of two to manage on a $27,500-a-year income. On very limited occasions (case by case) Stewardship for Life becomes intimately involved with people or families we believe have a suitable buoyancy of attitude, character, and the capacity for change. Such is the cause we are presently raising money for, known internally as "The Melissa Project."

Back to you. What if you decide at age 40 or 50 that you're too old to benefit from embracing stewardship of your limited resources—then you accidently live another 40 years? Even if you feel you're already living a pinched existence, aside from raising income or lowering expenses, there is little hope of improvement. Even if you are in what Stewardship for Life has termed *the pinch zone* earning 25,000 to 30,000 dollars per year (second quintile of income earners in Ohio) unless you find a way to right-size your spending-to-income ratios, there is little chance of moving forward. More education and/or training can help, but only if you **do not** ratchet up expenses and debt as you go forward.

I was able to break the inertia of generational poverty. My dad died when I was 11, and I was raised by my mom, who could not work because of her precarious health. So far, from my litter I am the only one to graduate from college (B.S. age 37, MBA age 50). My song "Bad at School" recounts some of my experiences (part of enhanced audio version). If it will serve the mission of Stewardship for Life and help alleviate generational poverty, I plan to leverage where I am into a doctorate degree, most likely in Leadership and Workforce Development. Fortunately for me, I am a huge fan of lifelong learning.

My very exceptional wife, Nita, went to law school in her forties and is in her sixth year of practice at a major downtown firm. She grew up in a middle-class, blue-collar, two-parent family, and I am fortunate to be associated with them. I know it is not in vogue to love your mother- and father-in-law, but I do.

I write of my experience not to brag; finishing an MBA 25 years after "normal" folks do is not terribly noble. My purpose is for example. My undergrad degree cost less than $1,200 (mostly testing fees). I read books and tested out of most topics. I got my MBA the old-fashioned way, four hours every Thursday night for two years (with 15 or 20 hours of studying each week).

Walking across the stage to receive a doctorate degree at age 60 or 61 will be a major life goal crossed off my list. The truth is, until I found a way to make a doctorate fit into my overall life mission, it was not important enough to expend the time and resources. Stewardship for Life will be my major vocational focus going forward. My message to you, dear reader, is to ***right-size your income to spending*** so you may have the flexibility to find work you love, ***and find a way to work with people you love.***

Apparently I have a recessive do-gooder gene. I've discovered it brings me lasting joy to help others in a way that actually empowers them rather than make them dependant on handouts. I am an *ah-ha!* junkie and thrive on the pleasure of finding and sharing small epiphanies. As a sometimes speaker/teacher, seeing that look of sudden understanding on a student's face is a real payoff. I believe that giving can be coupled with learning and understanding, and in a classier way than "you must listen to the sermon before you eat." Sometimes giving is just giving, and at some levels and needs (food and shelter), it should be *just giving*, but *giving* can be strategically designed to radically improve the long-term interest of the beneficiary. To me, the best reason to lower your burn rate (Hanson, 2007 Ch. 3), and square away your financial life is so that you may do "good work," as termed by Howard Gardner and Friends in *Good Work: When Excellence and Ethics Meet* (Gardner, Csikszentmihlyi, Damon, 2001).

In *Boundless Potential* Mark Walton (Walton,2012) provides an excellent guide for midlife and beyond, but would also be a great guide for finding meaningful work even if you are only in your second or third decade.

The real win of embracing "Good Stewardship" is the person you become, the freedom it provides, and the ability to *voluntarily* help those you wish to (even if it's only your family; every self-sustaining family unit is a big win for society at large). It's not the wealth you gain—it's the self-actualizing possibilities that will be available to you, the chance to do something in life that matters deeply to you and those you love. We are back to Keller and Papason: find that "one thing." Brendon Burchard is famous for saying that at the end of life, we will all ask ourselves three questions (Burchard, 2007). Having sat with two of my best friends in hospice situations I can tell you that Brendon is spot on. His three questions:

1. **Did I Live?**
2. **Did I Love?**
3. **Did I Matter?**

In the home study audio, you may hear a version of *Did I Matter* (Hanson, 2011), based on these questions, that I wrote for my late friend David Bennett while he was in hospice.

Do:
• Live a life of purpose
• Love what you do & who you do it with!
• Matter, in your life & others'
SFL
STEWARDSHIP FOR LIFE
To have:
great answers
at lifes end.
• Did I Live?
• Did I Love?
• Did I Matter?

Beginning with the end in mind, I have flipped Brendon's script by making a list of what you will need to do to have the answers to Brendon's questions at life's close.

My statements:

1. **Live a life of purpose**
2. **Love what you do and who you do it with**
3. **Find a way to deeply matter in your life and others'**

Notice that none of the promise of stewardship involves walking on hot coals or self-adulation in the mirror each morning. Rather, it involves the daily practice (TDP) of installing valuable habits (catch or create, train and release) and the operation of right-sizing spending to income. We are composed of a bundle of habits, and it's these habits—not willpower or chanting—that make us who we are. Of course, if you like hot coals or chanting at yourself in the mirror, go for it.

> *Quick rant*: Willpower can never trump habit. When you hear someone parrot "Where there is a will, there is a way," think *B.S.* I say, "Where there is a will, there is an impending death." Willpower is weak, habit is strong. Use scarce willpower to build habits.
>
> Think beyond popular memes. One of the most destructive memes I can think of is: "I've tried everything!" For starters, it is mathematically impossible to try everything, and if you try not quitting, the statement belies itself. Simply not quitting is often insanity—although, if you continue to fail after a reasonable time, a slight change of direction may be in order. Turn the right habits loose on problems, and they can work in the background without management.

There are few things in life as fulfilling and satisfying as knowing you are making daily progress on objectives you feel are worthwhile. Indeed, knowing that you have accepted responsibility for where you are in life, and not wasting time on excuses, is in itself liberating. Can you ever find a way to profit from blaming others for things that are actually your own fault (unless you are a politician)?

Although it may be not evident by looking at me, for the past year I have done at least 100 pushups (2 sets of 50) each day. Even after a year it still never seems like a good idea. But I have trained a habit, so I just hit the floor and begin. I have 15 or 20 done by the time I've finished trying to talk myself out of it. My goal is 10,000 steps a day (fitbit.com) and 100 pushups. If my system were more complicated, I probably would not be in my second year of this program.

This is what you have to do to install your stewardship habits or any habit you are trying to overwrite. **The best exercises, financial or physical, are the ones you will stick with.** Physically, you have weight resistance and aerobic training. Financially, the basics are spending control and debt elimination. (Review Chapter 3-Burn Rate)

We have to be in touch with our inner drill sergeant now and then. No one loves the drill sergeant while he's working, but the reflexive actions he drills into you may save your life on the battlefield one day. If you create and train your own drill sergeant as a firm but no-nonsense leader, he may well save your *physical and financial* life.

In early 2006, while driving home from a radio interview during my book tour, I had a mild heart attack. It took a long time to get my confidence and strength back after rehab, much to my dismay, over the next few years I allowed myself to gain more than 30 pounds. Then in 2012, something great happened to me. I decided to live. I took action to get in shape and pursue some of the lofty goals I had set in my Personal Development Plan, a ten-year-plan for self-improvement (created in MBA 701 in 2006).

With forward progress the halo effect kicks in, and good habits began to attract other good habits. As I lost weight, I became interested in living a life of purpose. Eventually I lost 62 pounds (current net loss of 54).

My point here is that the same principle will operate for you whether your burden is *physical or fiscal*. **I promise** that improving these areas in your life will make many other areas in your life better.

Jon Hanson, April 2, 2014

P.S. I hope you will enjoy this guide as much as I did creating it. Financial stability is the first step in creating a life of significance. Live, Love, Matter.

Whether:

- **Generational**
- **Situational** or
- **Self-inflicted**

Good Debt, Bad Debt Workbook

Introduction

1. Average millionaires, or those on the way to becoming so, save or invest _____ percent of their incomes.

   a) 10 to 15
   b) 15 to 20
   c) 20 to 30
   d) 40 to 50

Answer: (b) 15 to 20 percent. Meanwhile, average Americans spend 18 percent of their disposable income on consumer debt payments while saving little or nothing. In this sad juxtaposition lies a key premise of this book: "The past is the past—unless, of course, you still owe for it." Many can't start up the hill of financial freedom because they are carrying a backpack full of debt. (P. xxi)

Quick rant: The 15 to 18 percent we spend on CRAP could make us very wealthy over a 10- to 20-year period.

2. According to recent studies, what is most closely linked to wealth accumulation?

   a) a large income
   b) an inheritance
   c) willingness to plan
   d) frequent purchase of lottery tickets

Answer: (c) Willingness to plan, as determined by economists from New York University. A large income is not necessarily a guarantee of wealth. Nor is an inheritance. It can soon be frittered away. On the other hand, income of almost any size, when strained through ***well-trained habits***, can create wealth. (P. xxiii)

Quick rant: If you read the intro, you may see a theme about the importance of using your limited willpower to train habits. If you don't believe willpower is a limited resource, are you more or less patient after spending an hour listening to someone complain? For me, it's less.

3. Which of the following are important steps toward financial success? (circle all that apply)

   a) manage emotions

b) work from a plan
c) delay gratification
d) save/invest for your future

Answer: All of the above. Put these fundamentals to work in your life as a financial liturgy, and you will finish financially ahead of 97 percent of Americans. (P. xxvi)

Quick rant: Studies from Employee Benefit Research Institute indicate that 66 percent of Americans are not saving enough for retirement. The 3 percent is an elite group. The 1 percent, the bane of the Occupy Movement, actually starts at about $388,000 a year—not a millions of dollars a year, as popularly portrayed.

Q&A Chapter 1- The Debt Effects, the Invisible Hand of Debt

4. Who reaps the most benefits from our society's spending culture: consumers or merchants?

Answer: Merchants. For those who collect the money, America's spending culture is rewarding. Every purchase helps to keep their coffers overflowing. For those doing the spending, however, it is enslaving. (page 2)

5. Those who live in a constant state of ______ become slaves to their own passions.

a) need
b) want
c) hope
d) Nevada

Answer: (b) Want. There is a difference between needs and wants. Controlling our wants is one of the keys to financial success. (P. 3)

Quick rant: Certainly the use of debt can "take the waiting out of wanting," but as I've often said, "debt more often leaves us wanting." An irrefutable law is that you will always get more of what you subsidize. When we give life to our unbridled desires by feeding them, they grow larger, more dependent, and a huge drain on the host (that is you, dear reader.)

It's hard to give your heart to Jesus, when your butt belongs to Mastercard!

Q&A Chapter 2- Emotional Hostage: How Do I Get Free From Me?

25. Successful advertising generally relies on the customer's _________.

a) income
b) knowledge
c) emotions
d) taste in music

Answer: (c) The main ingredient in advertising is emotion. It's the spoonful of sugar that helps you swallow a lot of things that aren't good for you. Most every bad debt decision starts wrapped in the warm glow of emotion. (P. 36)

26. True or false: Advertising claims are generally trustworthy, especially when they come from a successful company.

Answer: False. If you allow yourself to be "educated" by sound bites and attractive models in ads or even network news, instead of rational thinking and study, you will be forever at the mercy of your emotions. The sales pitches for your money can be designed to make absolute sense, but when you strip all of the rhetoric away, the only question you need to ask yourself is whether this spending brings you nearer to or farther from your goals. (P. 37)

27. Who does advertising work best on?

a) the rich
b) the poor
c) those without a plan
d) those who own at least one margarita maker

Answer: (c) Those without a plan—although people who own gadgets for making just one kind of drink may well be more susceptible. In all seriousness, advertisers can easily gain your attention when you are not on a mission. The Econowise set an agenda and stick to it while shopping and managing their money. Advertising, public relations and all manner of propaganda works. If you see an infomercial run more than once, you can be assured it is at least pulling in enough to pay for the airtime and operators. (P. 37)

28. To become wealthy, you must go through a period of ______.

a) luck

b) debt
c) sacrifice
d) self-indulgence

Answer: c) Sacrifice. The right kind of sacrifice produces the great feeling you get when you promise yourself you will do something and refuse to quit until it is finished. It is possible to be born into wealth, or inherit it (although not with my family) but this is the exception rather than the rule. (P. 38)

29. Without control of your emotions and a definite plan, you leave your future to _______.

Answer: Chance. Do nothing, and you may be left to the financial plan Madison Avenue provides—which is to spend, spend, spend. You deserve a break today? Got $5 left? Come on in! (P. 38)

30. Which of these emotions do advertisers use to win customers? (circle all that apply)

a) fear
b) greed
c) jealousy
d) the desire to be safe
e) the desire to be loved or accepted

Answer: All of the above. However valid or attractive, all of these emotions and more can dull our common sense—making us think with our hearts rather than our heads. (P. 41)

31. Fundamentals are principles that act in a _______ manner independent of your understanding, action, or inaction.

a) consistent
b) profitable
c) damaging
d) geometric

Answer: (a) Consistent. Fundamentals are time tested and proved by common sense. Being successful means knowing and applying healthy fundamentals, such as spending less than you make. Duh!? (P. 45)

32. The main difference between the Consumerati and the Econowise is their view of what?

a) the future
b) the market
c) other people
d) the TV screen

Answer: (a) The future. The Consumerati believe in what they can see and touch now. They have little confidence in tomorrow—which is why they're so willing to pledge or mortgage it. The Consumerati seek immediate happiness, even if it's only temporary. The Econowise seek lasting joy. (P. 50)

At Stewardship for Life many of the people we seek to help, whether supporter or participant, have not had any training in financial matters. The material we publish generally will fall into one of these four realms:

- Financial Literacy
- Attitude Management
- Communication/Non-Sales Selling
- Preparing a Written PDP, Personal Development Plan. We require participants to put together a written plan spanning ten years or more into the future. For program participants, we provide coaching and career assessment testing.

33. Freedom is found in:

a) a 1967 Corvette convertible
b) a long line of credit
c) home ownership
d) self-discipline

Answer: (d) Self-discipline (although classic car enthusiasts might take issue with this one.) This is counter to everything popular culture teaches you, but freedom is found in restraint. Only through conscious choice can we begin to control our outcomes. When we become slaves to our feelings, our actions are at the mercy of our moods, our money, available credit, or the urging of an advertiser. (P. 50)

Q&A Chapter 3- Burn Rate: Spending. Not Income, Determines Wealth

34. True or false: Spending is not a problem as long as all of your existing needs and

many desires are being met.

Answer: False. For some, a job that provides for all their present needs may give them the illusion of wealth. Mix this together with a little easy-to-get consumer debt, and present needs or desires seem to expand. Just as work tends to expand to the time allotted, spending, without restraint, expands to the amount of money available—or even beyond. The tendency to confuse income with wealth is near an epidemic level among Americans. Income is like a moving river; wealth is like a lake or reservoir. Stored income is wealth, while spent income may not even bring fond memories. (P. 54)

35. What is a burn rate?

a) your fixed cost of existence
b) the rate of interest accumulation on credit card debt
c) how fast you can swipe your debit card at the register
d) the number of miles you have to run to work off a cheeseburger

Answer: (a) Your fixed cost of existence. Burn rate is the actual amount of money you spend each month to stay in the same place—your status quo. This includes all fixed costs of living and the impulse buying you do now and then. It's all the money spent that does not increase your wealth—that which is consumed and gone forever. (P. 55)

36. If you are now forty years old, every $100 monthly you burn (spend) knocks out _________ of potential retirement nest egg.

a) $132
b) $1,320
c) $13,200
d) $132,000

Answer: (d) You read that right: an extra $100 spent monthly on beer, dining out, or a deluxe cable package could end up costing you $132,000 in your retirement years. (P. 58)

37. What percentage of folks at retirement age are partially or totally dependent on government or family?

a) 40%
b) 60%
c) 90%
d) 120%

Answer: (c) It may seem shocking, but 90% of Americans are not self-sufficient in retirement. You'll reach retirement age (or early death) someday. By that time, you can hope that social security is still an option or your kids have enough extra wealth to support you. Or you can plan ahead. (P. 59)

38. True or false: Regardless of where you're at financially now, you can always make more money.

Answer: False. Eventually you will run out of time or energy to make the money you need. While you are young and healthy, yes, you can make more money, but the clock is still running out on you. In time, the optimism of youth must give way to the physical body of old age. As Arnold Bennett stated, "Which of us has not been saying to himself all his life: 'I shall alter that when I have a little more time'?" As you get older, you may notice that you begin to value time more than money. (P. 65)

39. It is your __________, not your income, that will determine your fate.

a) burn rate
b) interest rate
c) college degree
d) movie star looks

Answer: (a) Your burn rate as a percentage of income is the most accurate predictor of your eventual success or failure financially. This fundamental is as sure as gravity and as certain as earthly death. Spending, more than earnings, is the problem for most Americans. If you redirect your income to take care of your future, after a time you can have your heart's desires from the earnings of your investments. (P. 70)

Your Burn Rate Determines Your Fate!

Q&A Chapter 4- Delayed Gratification: Don't Wait to Get It!

40. To "delay gratification" is to:

a) put off a purchase until it fits into your financial plan
b) charge a purchase to a lower-interest-rate credit card
c) avoid your creditors for as long as possible
d) save the kiss for the second date

Answer: Okay, this was a trick question. The answers are A and D, but A is the one I want to talk about. (I'll leave D to you and your sweetie. Be different and wait until the third date.) The interesting thing about applying delayed gratification is that over time, many of your wants will change. Recall Lord Byron's words: "The lovely toy so fiercely sought hath lost its charm by being caught." (P. 79)

41. The opposite of delayed gratification is ________.

a) currency
b) immediacy
c) agency
d) idiocy

Answer: (b) immediacy. You are falling into the trap of immediacy if you are spending money in order to appear wealthy. The money that many people spend to appear wealthy could instead make them actually wealthy with time and patience. Now that I think about it, *idiocy* might work, too. Give yourself a half point if you chose (d). (P. 90)

42. True or false: Excuses can temporarily soothe the awful reality that we are where we are because of our own choices.

Answer: True. Many blame the government, taxes, discrimination, big business, or anything that suits them. For some, this avoidance technique can last for a lifetime. It can be easier to ignore that we failed to plan than to believe that our whole philosophy of life is wrong. Many of us hate to admit that we've followed the pied piper of consumerism to an unpleasant end. But what can't be avoided are the financial repercussions of our choices. (P. 82)

43. While both the Consumerati and the Econowise labor and earn money, only the ________ add to the pool of capital available to everyone.

Answer: Econowise. All capital comes from the labor of the savers/investors among the Econowise. Labor comes in the form of brain work or back work; capital comes from labor; and stored labor is capital—stocks, bonds, notes and mortgages, real estate, and cash savings. Without the Econowise, the Consumerati would have little capital to borrow. (P. 83)

Mr. Johnson, we cannot make you the loan and, we'd like to have our calendar back...

44. True or false: Converting bad debt to a real estate loan can turn it into good debt.

Answer: False. Debt that replaces debt—though perhaps on different terms—is nevertheless debt. Don't allow yourself to be fooled by the semantic deceptions so common in today's advertising and media. You must take charge of how you sort and use the words that come to you. Separate the words from your emotion. (P. 85)

45. You can calculate your reality income by dividing your net worth by the number of _________.

a) dollars you owe
b) credit cards you own
c) years you have worked
d) pizzas you can eat in one sitting

Answer: (c) Years you have worked. Your reality (or real) income is how much you are working for per year. No matter how much you make a year, only what adds to your net worth is yours. If you have a net worth of $150,000 and have worked for twenty years, you are in fact working for $7,500 per year. The rest has been burned. Ouch! (P. 89)

46. _______________ is the death of every wealth-building program.

a) A loss in wages
b) A high credit card interest rate
c) The inability to delay gratification
d) The Democratic Party
e) The Republican Party
f) Any politician

Answer: (c) Perhaps the most damaging aspect of today's culture is short-term thinking: "I want it all and I want it now!" The uninformed are always at the mercy of the merchants of the world. Herbert Spencer wrote, "The chief difference between the savage and civilized man is civilized man's ability to think and plan ahead for another day." Yet many of us choose to live like savages, never thinking of tomorrow. Our refusal to delay our immediate desires finds us ultimately with a fraction of what we could rightfully claim. (P. 76, 90)

47. In matters of saving and investing, sooner is better but __________.

a) later will work out eventually.
b) tomorrow is okay too.
c) budgeting is hard.
d) even sooner is best.

Answer: (d) Even sooner is best. When we decide to wait to begin our plan, rationalizing that we will start being thrifty and wise another day, we are really saying, "Just give me the leftovers of life." Discipline delayed is discipline denied. Compound interest needs time. The investments of youth are ever more fertile than the investments of the older person. (P. 90)

The late Barney Zick used to say, "Sooner is better, but more sooner is best!"

Q&A Chapter 5 – I Don't Know About My Past, But My Future is Spotless.

48. True or false: If your past has many events where lack of money is the central focus, then how you "use" these events as you recall them will affect your philosophy of money.

Answer: True. Many people like to think that the past doesn't matter, but as long as it is a glowing ember, it probably does. For me, it altered my ability to delay gratification. I was always eager to rush ahead, trying to outpace my white trash past. (P. 99)

49. True or false: Your childhood environment affects the kind of life you will lead.

Answer: True. Well, at least, initially. If you're born in a good neighborhood, you may have a better life than if you're raised in a poor part of town. If you're able to understand the lessons you picked up from your past, however, you may do very well, even if you are a boy or girl from Hardscrabble. Conversely, we've all seen those who seem to have every advantage but are unable to become wealthy, or dribble away wealth that was given to them. (P. 106)

50. It is best to use your past as a ____________.

a) place to live
b) reference library
c) script for your life
d) basis for a tell-all autobiography

Answer: (b) reference library, although (d) could be fun too, especially if it increases your cash flow. Use your past as a reference library—not a place to live. My book-marketing mentor Mark Victor Hansen says, "You are not born a winner or a loser, you are born a chooser." You may operate with the mindset of a resident of Hardscrabble or the mindset of a Park Avenue blue blood. (P. 106)

Off script: Twisted Scripture from the NRV (New Redneck Version) 1st Hesitations 4:11-14 [11]: "Poor folks are plentiful, so help them anytime you wish. However, you will not always have the opportunity to help yourself.[12] The best way to help the poor is to not be one of them.[13] This, my brother or sister, is not an invitation to stinginess but a call to stewardship, plan, save, work, and so act in a way to better your lot in life and be in the position to help others.[14] Thou shalt feed and clothe your brethren but not provideth him a big screen TV."

51. ________ can hurt you financially from the distraction alone, and is hard on you both mentally and physically.

a) Hopes and dreams
b) Bitterness
c) Self-control
d) New York Style Cheesecake

Answer: (b) Bitterness over mistakes, failures, or past experiences will never achieve anything. The sooner you can dump it, the better off you will be financially and personally. (P. 107)

As for cheesecake, it can be hard on the waistline but is too delicious to give up entirely.

52. It is important to take __________ of our efforts rather than indulge in pity, envy, and jealousy.

a) a Facebook poll
b) an Instagram photo
c) a realistic inventory
d) an optimistic evaluation

Answer: (c) A realistic inventory. It will always be easier to support a "cause" or vote for someone who promises to "make things better" than to actually apply personal effort to make things better for yourself. As a TV comedian once said, "It's a long, hard climb to the middle." Laugh, but do climb to the middle. It's on the way to the top, and it's so much nicer than the bottom. (P. 108)

53. The choice we have when faced with life's adversities is always to become

____________.

a) wealthy or healthy
b) strong or strung out
c) better or buttery
d) bitter or better

Answer: (d) Bitter or better. After a difficult period in life, bitterness may seem like the most reasonable and economical choice in the beginning. Yet to become better is the more profitable route in the long term. Will we drag the past along or leave it in the reference library? Will we learn the lessons of life or repeat over and over the same mistakes? This is your life, not a test run. Change is within everyone's grasp. (P. 108)

Off script: If you have the enhanced version of the *Good Debt, Bad Debt* audio produced by Stewardship for Life, listen to the song "Both Ends" (by yours truly). I wrote this at the end of 2011. I had Jay Speight of Nashville produce and sing. I do (sing/talk) only very obvious comedy. It was my year-end reflection song. Most of the songs I have included with this package are family, life, love, loss, and financial literacy. Songs such as "Best Return" and "Credit Card Junkie" are meant to entertain and teach. Songs like "Real Soldierman," "Daughter of Mine," and "A Father's Eyes" are meant to remind us that, as important as finances are, there are ultimately more important things. Yet we must also grasp that proceeding in the right direction will enhance and amplify those things in life we value more than money.

54. What has the power to pull the past into your present and future, and keep on affecting it? (Other than family, of course.)

Answer: Debt. Remember, the past is the past unless you still owe for it. (P. 109)

Q&A Chapter 6 - What if You Live?

55. True or false: Success in retirement comes more from starting and sticking to a plan than from the actual investment.

Answer: True. Unless you were born wealthy, to retire comfortably you will serve a period of financial sacrifice. The well-trained mind sees this time period as a blessing and not a sacrifice. The earlier you start, the less severe the pain and the shorter the sacrifice. (P. 112)

Other: The best investment is one you will stick to and add to weekly or monthly. Remember, you are operating a 20- or 50-year plan (yours might even be longer).

56. True or false: Our chances for success are better with a complex plan that we sometimes follow than a simple system that we always follow.

Answer: False. John Bogle, founder of Vanguard Mutual Funds, explains, "Simplicity gives us the power to do less of what doesn't matter—and gives us the power to do more of what does matter." Limiting options sounds like the wrong advice, doesn't it? Yet most would agree that picking the right option and sticking with it is a good limitation. (P. 113)

57. To apply thrift to your life, you must ________.

a) spend
b) plan
c) have a large income
d) start with some debt

Answer: (b) Plan. You must have a written program to follow. Without such a plan, life is inefficient and costly. Thrift assumes forethought and careful reasoning. A large income is not necessarily an indicator of wealth. An income of almost any size strained through well-trained habits in time will create wealth. (P. 114)

58. If you have debt and low savings, paying a monthly cable TV bill or payments on an expensive car is like paying a voluntary ____.

Answer: Tax. Ben Franklin once said, "The cost of one vice can support two children." I think old Ben was onto something here. We should tax ourselves, not for vice, but for our futures. Redistribute the money from your cigarette habit, cable bill, or DVD budget to a more worthy cause: you and your family. The best way to "collect" the tax from yourself is to use the government's approach—deduct it first and often, and by electronic transfer from your paycheck or checking account to a prudent investment. The automation of the deposits is key. (P. 117)

59. The most difficult part of a plan is usually ____________.

a) the beginning
b) the brainstorming
c) the day-to-day application
d) telling your spouse

Answer: (c) The day-to-day application. We may start a plan with great enthusiasm, and then get bogged down in the details and drudgery that must be worked through for success. Sticking to the day-to-day commitment is crucial to making your financial plan work. (P. 119)

60. Most of us fail by ignoring ________.

a) the big things.
b) the small things.
c) the things that go bump in the night.
d) anything plaid.

Answer: (b) The small things. Longfellow wrote, "Most people would succeed in small things if they were not troubled with great ambitions." The simple daily duties of life are really the building blocks of our greater ambitions. (P. 120)

We have a special policy on Harold, it pays off if, he COMES to life...

61. To be successful, we must avoid the great disconnect between _________.

a) knowing and doing
b) doing and watching TV
c) ourselves and our mothers
d) good budgets and bad budgets

Answer: (a) Knowing and doing. (Although you may find that some of these other disconnects are also problematic.) Many people long for a better life, yet head in the other direction mentally. Some of us read and study for years, thinking a little more knowledge is all we need to reach the Promised Land. Those who hold knowing to be equal to doing are forever lost. Some never turn graduation day into application day, when we apply what we have learned. The learning process is so satisfying for some that they fear stepping into the real world. (P. 124)

62. The more you dislike your job, the more motivation you should have to lower your ______ and increase savings.

a) expectations
b) aspirations
c) burn rate
d) income

Answer: (c) Burn rate. You'll be in a better position to switch jobs or quit if you lower your burn rate and increase savings. If you don't, you probably aren't serious about changing jobs. In the few years prior to 1981 when I left my "secure job," I had drastically lowered my burn rate and increased savings. Even though my first year in real estate amounted to a severe cut in pay, my expenses were so low that it really was not a problem. (P. 126)

63. One quick rule of thumb for determining how much you'll need for retirement is to take the desired amount per year you need to retire in today's dollars and multiply it by ____.

a) 3
b) 10
c) 40
d) 100

Answer: (c) 40. If you want $30,000 per year in today's dollars, you need to put back $1.2 million. If you want $50,000 per year, plan on putting back $2 million. This calculation can be quite eye-opening. It's clear that the longer you wait, the amount you'll have to save will be that much greater. (P. 130)

Quick rant: Unless you can accurately manage and predict a realistic outcome of your investments, it may be wise to talk to a Certified Financial Planner. A fee-based planner is often best. The Gardner Brothers at Motley Fool have many articles about this type of service (www.fool.com)

64. If you pay $1 a day ($30 a month) into your wealth insurance program from birth

to age sixty-five, you will have over _________ if your 65-year average rate of return is 10 percent.

a) $250,000
b) $500,000
c) $1 million
d) $2 million

Answer: (d) $2 million. Yep, just $1 a day can become $2 million with the right commitment to saving (and a parent willing to start a fund for you). It's clear that the savings habit is more important than the rate of return (yield). (P. 132)

65. True or false: Writing down your goals is an essential part of the financial journey.

Answer: True. Why do people hesitate to write down their goals on paper or in a journal? Because writing something down makes it real. Reality can be harsh. When we are making little progress or even regressing, we often allow ourselves a free pass by not documenting reality. In the end, though, becoming the type of person who can achieve your goals is more important than just writing them down. (P. 133)

Updated advice: In addition to my advice on goal setting, I would read *The One Thing* (Keller & Papason, 2011). It offers excellent updated research and is one of the best books I have read on productivity. I have really enjoyed this book and believe it to be well worth the money. I have the audible version on my Droid and the hardcover book. Money well spent. *I rarely recommend any book with such enthusiasm.* The habits section alone is worth the price of entry. **Thank you, Gary Keller and Jay Papason**, for this well researched valuable information.

66. Which is more likely to cause us to make poor choices: contentment or discontent?

Answer: Discontent. It often causes us to do things for the wrong reasons. Through the calm lenses of contentment and reason, we are able to make wise choices. If you're about to make a spending decision, back up a bit. Take a long-term look at your current short list of desires. Do they fit into your long-term plan? (P. 137)

67. The true cost of a thing is ____________________.

a) the amount on the price tag
b) the amount you pay after haggling with the salesman
c) the amount of life you are willing to give up to pay for it
d) the amount of time you will spend arguing with your spouse about it

Answer: (c) The amount of life you're willing to give up to pay for it. Each time you make a purchase, you are paying not only with money, but with the amount of time you spent working to make that money. Buckminster Fuller, according to Brian Tracy, wrote, "Wealth is the number of days you can exist without working." This is the most useful definition of wealth I have heard. (P. 139)

68. Disposable income since the 1950s has ____________.

a) increased by half
b) increased nearly threefold
c) decreased nearly threefold
d) decreased by half

Answer: (b) Disposable income has increased nearly threefold even when adjusted for inflation. Yet we have expanded our desires so quickly that we miss the opportunity to take care of ourselves first and be free. Our increase in disposable income since the 1950s has largely been wasted. Instead of investing for our futures, we lust after every consumer gadget and convenience known to man. (P. 140)

69. Retirement wealth is primarily a product of time, accumulation, and _______.

a) luck
b) optimism
c) discipline
d) shuffleboard scores

Answer: (c) Discipline. Luck may sometimes play a part, but for most of us it's far from the top three. Planning, or goal setting, with a knowable beginning, middle, and end, is the preeminent tool for success. (P. 140)

Other: Make savings a habit as early in life as you can, and the savings habit will save you.

Q&A Chapter 7- Real Estate

70. Your eventual success or failure in real estate will hinge on your ability to find and recognize _______.

Answer: a bargain. You may accidentally make some money in real estate, but the odds are against it. Whether your real estate market is heading up or down, being able to discern value is the only way to profit from it. In the past, cash was king; today common sense is king. Bargains are out there, but you are not facing an entire market ready to sell for cents on the dollar. It may take a while to find the bargains. (P. 141)

Real estate rant: Success in real estate hinges on VALUE, LEVERAGE, and USE. There are other forms of leverage—debt leverage is one. The use of debt on real estate is best kept below 67 percent of a sane value based on the expected quick sale price. Other ways to leverage real estate include the following:

- changing use
- control through options
- control by purchasing debt (even low or nonperforming)
- leasing
- granting or acquiring easements
- vertical breakups
- air rights
- creative deed restrictions
- obtaining bankruptcy claims
- collecting judgments
- tax deeds
- becoming a substituted plaintiff in a foreclosure for a fee
- acquiring debt at an extreme discount and modifying terms (be aware that you might lose the priority of your position if your modification impairs the value of a junior lien holder)
- discount sale leasebacks
- buying just a payment stream
- buying a remainder
- obtaining an option on the whole—in exchange for buying a partial or loaning money (how Wayne Huizenga came to own the Miami Dolphins, a loan on Joe Roby Stadium)
- buy within a retirement plan or IRA to defer gain
- collapsible wrap-arounds
- AITDs
- land contracts
- subordination for a fee
- partial subordination
- leveraged buyout of a property by obtaining assignments of a majority of the debt (keep title deed in a separate entity)
- accelerating your senior loan to force junior lien holders to pay up or cut short at sale practically any combination of the above

I did most of the above for about ten years. It does expand the mind when looking at real estate. I used to say I was in the "debt arbitrage" business. I expect this experience will help me handle real estate, liens, mortgages, and other noncash "gifts" for the benefit of Stewardship for Life.

71. If you want to buy a house, stop talking and start ____.

a) walking
b) writing
c) waiting
d) wiggling

Answer: (b) Writing. Make sure you can discern the value, and then write the offer down and hand it to the seller. If you have no training, get some professional advice from a competent broker or real estate attorney. He can help you with the proper contingencies, such as a financing and home inspection. I once wrote 71 offers before getting an offer for 50 percent of asking price accepted. For one thing, I didn't need a house, and I had cash. Realtors hate when I mention this story. (P. 146)

72. True or false: When purchasing real estate, your success rate will be higher if you prearrange your funding for the purchase.

Answer: True. With your funding in hand, make your offer plain and simple, and avoid overloading your contracts with contingencies. All sellers want the most money, the quickest sale, and the fewest problems. I say give them two out of three: quickest sale and fewest problems. (P. 146)

73. What should you do if you lose a deal on a home by making too low of an offer?

a) Call the seller repeatedly with a higher offer until you get a response.
b) Let the seller know that he has lost out on the perfect buyer.
c) Bid higher on the next home.
d) Be polite and move on.

Answer: (d) Be polite and move on. You may have to make offers on many homes before you find the right bargain. **The ones that get away will never hurt you.** (P. 147)

The best attitude is: "Next!"

74. If you have an income problem, you can address it through the three Es. What are they?

a) earnings, ear-marking, and econometrics

b) education, efficiency, and emotion
c) education, effort, and enterprise
d) earnings, effort, and entropy

Answer: (c) Education, effort, and enterprise. These apply to real estate too, except that you have a product you may live in while tackling all three steps. (P. 148)

75. True or false: It is generally the condition of the real estate market that determines your chances of making a great profit.

Answer: False. It's the human element that matters here. Real estate is a people business. You buy real estate from people, it gets used or rented by people, and when you sell it, you must entice another human or entity to pay money to you. Become proficient in valuing houses in the area you want to live, and work on your people skills. (P. 149)

Other: In 2010 I bought a warehouse from a $3.15 billion dollar company, #145 on the list of Forbes private companies. The deal still came down to my ability to communicate with "people." People deal with people they like.

76. What are the three tests to determine if a real estate investment is good debt?

a) value, leverage, and use
b) equity, principal, and income
c) escrow, margin, and depreciation
d) litmus, paternity, and I.Q.

Answer: (a) Value, leverage, and use. *Test one*: Does the value of your purchase exceed the loan by a safe margin? *Test two*: Will the loan self-amortize through the use, rental, operation, or resale of operating or reselling the asset? Are the terms beneficial to you? *Test three*: Is the item for income, resale, or utility? Do you even need this item? Will it add to or subtract from your net worth? Is this something you can handle? Based on use, income, or resale, is it profitable? (P. 150)

77. True or false: Forced inflation is one key to making money in real estate.

Answer: True. Forced inflation can come by way of sweat equity (you improve the property by making physical improvements) or by finding a bargain. (P. 151)

78. True or false: Buying property in an area where major road construction and population shifts occur is a bad idea.

Answer: False. Owning property in the path of progress may allow you to benefit from the increase in values driven by the demand for the area. This is most prevalent in commercial property, but residential housing may benefit also. This is an example of forced inflation, though it is inflation not driven by you. (P. 152)

I am one for two on this. My path of progress guesses aren't always that great. Some are obvious. We have land near a Kroger store (919 feet from the edge of town) with small warehouses and income, and we think that one will do well.

79. When a seller decides to knock 35 percent off the price of a house or other property, he wants to have his money quickly. Many are unable to take advantage of the opportunity because of ______.

Answer: Bad debt. When you see a great opportunity, it is unlikely that you will be able to take advantage of it if you have bad debt, because you will be financially unable to do so. **Funds already spoken for must remain silent when opportunity knocks.** (That's almost Zen, huh?) (P. 154)

80. If you are living rent-free (for instance, with your parents) and not saving as much as it would cost to rent a decent place, you are ___________.

a) sixteen
b) foolish
c) too clever by half
d) using the strategy outlined by economist Lei Z. Bumm

Answer: (b) Foolish. If you are eating out of Mommy's refrigerator and not paying rent or banking a majority of your earnings, you are training a vicious appetite that will someday bite you. If you cannot save 50 percent of your income while someone else feeds and shelters you, you are well on your way to a lifetime membership in the Consumerati. (P. 163)

81. An easily affordable home is one that ___________________________.

a) will get your children into the best public school
b) will consume 50% or less of your monthly income
c) can be purchased with an adjustable-rate mortgage
d) you can make payments on even if your income is cut in half

Answer: (d) In *The Millionaire Mind*, Tom Stanley discusses an "easily affordable home," defining it as one that you could easily make the payments on even if your income was cut in half. He goes further to say that if you have ever owned an easily affordable home and continue to do so, that is an indicator of your eventual success. (P. 164)

82. True or false: The best place to begin in real estate is with a starter home.

Answer: True. Popular culture teaches us to value comfort over sensibility and to buy the biggest and best, whether we can afford it or not. Statistically you're not likely to be in the home for even seven years. Success is at hand if you strive to put in the effort to profitably climb up from a rational beginning. (P. 165)

83. Generally, as a guideline for lenders, what percentage of your gross income is allowed for housing expenses?

a) 15%
b) 29%
c) 44%
d) 50%

Answer: (b) 29%. This can be moved as high as 41% if you do not have other debts. If you are earning $50,000 per year, you could have a housing expense of up to $1,200 a month. Depending on your taxes and insurance payments, this could put you in a $150,000 house when interest rates are 7%. (P. 165)

84. True or false: It's wiser to buy a house that's the right size and provide your own storage on-site rather than rent a storage unit.

Answer: Way True. Storage units often rent for as much as $14 per square foot per year (locally). A 10x10 mini storage unit for $85 a month or $1,020 a year goes for $10.20 per square foot. That $10.20 per square foot is a good start on building a garage. (P. 167)

85. What is it called when a builder or seller allows his bank to collect interest in advance, which is added to the cost of the loan to give you a low payment for the first few years?

a) buy down
b) buy up
c) buy-and-wait
d) bait-and-switch

Answer: (a) Buy down. Don't fall into the trap of a builder that buys down a rate for you and marks up the house to cover it. A buy-down is a gift you pay for. (P. 167)

Q&A Chapter 8 - Driving My Life Away

86. True or false: Debt for a car is usually good debt.

Answer: False. Car debt is a loan on something that decreases in value. Cars are commodities. For nearly two-thirds of Americans, cars represent a payment that is included in their burn rate. Until you can pay cash for your vehicles, the best advice is to keep the expense moderate. Even if you pay cash for your car, truck, or SUV, it still depreciates rapidly. (P. 170)

87. The average car depreciates at roughly $___ per month over three years.

a) $100
b) $175
c) $250
d) $400

Answer: (c) $250. This is the $250 that can make the difference between cat food and caviar in retirement. (P. 174)

88. If you redirect a typical monthly car payment of $383 to a retirement fund for ten years, it could add up to about ________.

a) $30,000
b) $46,000
c) $74,000
d) $110,000

Answer: (c) $74,000, based on 9% interest. Saving a few hundred bucks a month on car expenses may not be too exciting in the beginning, but once you have accumulated some savings, you can watch your net worth grow monthly from investments you direct. Again, the important part is starting and sticking to a plan. (P. 178)

89. If you are in debt or just want to do something smarter with your money, what is the simple solution to transportation?

a) Buy more and drive it less
b) Buy less and drive it longer
c) Buy big and think small
d) Buy big and sell early

Answer: (b) Buy less and drive it longer. Can you drive less of a car and have low or no payments? The short answer is yes. The more difficult answer is maybe—if you are willing to learn not to care about having the latest-model car with all the newest options. Remember, few things in life fade as quickly as the "new-car high." (P. 178)

90. What is the most popular color of car—and the one that is easiest to resell?

Answer: White. (Silver and black tie for second place.) You may be able to get a special deal on less desirable colors, like brown or green, but those may be more difficult to resell. (P. 184)

91. True or false: Depreciation impacts us only when we sell.

Answer: True. You should be particularly worried about depreciation, as to resale, if you plan to trade or sell in a few years. If you're selling, depreciation is undesirable; if you're buying, it may be a boon. It probably won't affect the daily drivability of the vehicle. (P. 184)

Quick rant: If the depreciation is a result of manufacturing or design mistakes—like the old Suzuki Samurais that dropped in value because they kept tipping over, or the Yugos because they Don't Go—those are different problems.

92. Sales representatives for credit card services commonly tell restaurant owners that patrons will spend up to ___ percent more when they can pay by credit card.

a) 10
b) 20
c) 30
d) 40

Answer: (d) 40 percent. Consumers spend far more when purchasing on credit. This principle applies to car purchases also. For most people, if they saved the amount it took to pay cash for the vehicle they think they want, when the time came to purchase it they would prefer to keep the cash rather than handing it over. If we allow a car salesperson or ourselves to position our decision as a $489 decision and not a $23,000 decision, we are being deceived. (P. 186)

Quick rant: Again, credit and debt distorts reality…

93. True or false: If you must finance a car, you should arrange your financing at the car dealership, where you're more likely to get the best deal.

Answer: False. Before going to the dealership, arrange your financing ahead of time with your bank or local credit union. Do the research about what you will pay and all of your fantasizing about the car before you go to buy it. This will give you time to realize it's just another car and to recall that your financial goals are more important than a car. If you skip this step, you may react to a counteroffer or agree to something you don't really want. (P. 187)

94. What is the ultimate weapon in negotiating for a car?

a) a large line of credit
b) a good credit score
c) the ability to say no
d) a well-formed spit wad

Answer: (c) The ability to "Just say no!" Make your offer, be polite, but be ready to walk. If you can't work it out, say, "Let me know if your circumstances change." Then get up and walk. Resist the manipulations that are sure to follow. (P. 188)

Car Salesman:

Salesman: What do I have to do to earn your business?
Me: Just get your heart right on the price.
Salesman: That's the best we can do.
Me: *Standing up*. Well, I don't want to waste your time. Let me know if your circumstances change.
Salesman: Don't you like the car?
Me: What's not to like? It's a new car.
Salesman: Think of the money you'll save in fuel alone.
Me: I did, and it's pretty small when I add back the cost of the vehicle, higher insurance, and financing or loss of interest on my savings.
Salesman: You'll never get a better deal than this on this car.
Me: Well, there are 265 Ford Dealers in the Southern Ohio Ford Dealers Association. Let me check with a few others. Have a nice day. I gotta get home—*Shark Tank* is on in 30 minutes. Do you ever watch that show?

The entire process is dependent on you not really having to have a car. Wanters and walkers are poor negotiators. Have some fun. Before you get to a dealer, new or used, make sure you have all the research and know a Black Book value or KBB.com dealer trade-in value, or if new, make sure you know the invoice costs and incentives or rebates in your area. Remember, the time and investment process wears them down the same as it does you. You have to be stronger. If you go through all this in ten minutes, they won't feel like they have much invested, but no one likes to work hard for 30 to 60 minutes and come up empty.

When you get the deal you want, they go for the nibble, listing how many free oil changes or add-on options they will throw in. Know more than the salesman about the car and the cost, and have your financing done (outside of the dealership) unless they have a deal that far exceeds what you can do at your bank. A friend who bought a new 2013 Honda Civic put 35 percent down, got zero interest for 60 months, and purchased $500 below invoice (last day of February).

95. True or false: Cars are commodities to be used, not investments.

Answer: True. Cars are continually depreciating. If you choose to buy an expensive car, it should be an income-appropriate expenditure purchased with the full realization of what else you could have done with that money. (P. 193)

Q&A Chapter 9 - Do I Have Records?

Can I get a receipt for that?

96. True or false: Poor record keeping will cost you only time in the long run.

Answer: False. Sloppy record keeping can cost individuals and companies hugely. The costs may come in the form of not claiming a tax deduction, paying a late fee, or losing an opportunity because you don't know your financial status, or just in pure frustration. Along this line, record keeping can mean more than just tracking the dollars. Recently I was looking for a survey for a piece of land to resell and could not find it. This not only caused a delay; I ultimately lost the sale. (P. 196)

97. True or false: Time spent on record keeping tends to increase your creative ability.

Answer: True. With accurate records, you give a measure of validity to planning and forecasting. A dose of reality can be a sobering pill, but without it you are merely building castles in the sky (or on paper). With accurate records you will be more powerful, since you'll have the information at hand. (P. 196)

98. True or false: It's cheaper and more accurate to keep records by hand using pencil and paper than to use a software program for the same purpose.

Answer: False. Buying a software program is an investment that will save you time and likely money as well. Not only are financial software applications quicker and more accurate, but many allow you to generate reports and comparisons you would never even conceive of doing by hand. (P. 209)

99. Which financial software program is recommended for efficient record-keeping in Chapter 9?

Answer: Quicken Home and Business. You can generate reports and even cool pie charts showing where the money went. Within a few months, you can easily have a very good picture of where every penny of your money goes. (P. 199)

Update: The best record keeping system to use is the one you will actually use. It doesn't matter if it's an old notebook or a sophisticated spreadsheet.

100. True or false: Spending without keeping good records is like flying VFR (visual flight rules) rather than IFR (instrument flight rules).

Answer: True. Without good records, you are flying with no fixed point of reference. Without a fixed point of reference, you are like a guy in a small plane who never really knows if his altimeter is correct. If you don't know how high above sea level you are, and the terrain in front of you is higher—well, you get the point. Yet many people fly daily without instruments. Flying VFR (visual flight rules) is great when the skies are clear and you can see the whole terrain. The worst thing you can do is to be flying VFR in IFR weather. Get instruments—in other words, Quicken or a similar record-keeping product. (P. 204)

101. It is best to start record keeping with a _______.

a) tax return
b) record of what you are currently spending
c) list of what you plan to spend in the next month
d) desk piled with random receipts, sticky notes, and empty take-out containers

Answer: (b) A record of what you are currently spending. Once you have a few months of expenses in your record system, you will automatically have a budget. It may not be a good one, but it will be an actual budget, not a budget of where you *think* you are. From there, you will be able to see where you can improve. (P. 205)

102. _________ is the money you spend but don't really think about, which can add up to a fortune over time.

a) the Latte Factor
b) the Millionaire Factor
c) the Max factor
d) the Human Factor

Answer: (a) The Latte Factor. This is the money you spend but don't really think about, which can add up to a fortune over time. The term was coined by David Back, author of *Finish Rich.* When you track your spending, you might be very surprised at how much you spend on takeout food or in many other seemingly insignificant areas. It's easy to saw through $300 to $600 or $1,000 a month in small, insignificant things. (P. 205)

103. What is a sinking fund?

a) the money wasted on random purchases
b) the cost of a new concrete foundation
c) a fund for expected expenses
d) a fund for boat repairs

Answer: (c) A sinking fund is a fund for *expected* expenses. If you know that an expense of $300 has to be paid every six months, you set aside $50 a month in anticipation of the payment. I have a friend who, although he doesn't have a car payment, has a sinking fund to replace his cars when the time comes. (P. 205)

104. Which tax software program is recommended in Chapter 9?

Answer: TurboTax. This program interviews you, asking about all the basic stuff: name, social security number, and so on. It simply takes the information and puts it in the correct boxes on the IRS forms. Later it will ask if you had any rental properties for the year, whether you pay child care, and if you have a small business. If you fill in the boxes correctly, TurboTax is more consistent and accurate than the pencil-chewing little guy I formerly used. (P. 206)

Tax rant: No matter what CPA you use, in the end your taxes are your responsibility. I had mine pretty screwed up in the early '90s, and it cost me a great deal (even with a CPA). Just remember, it's your body part in the audit ringer.

105. Your core desire to be successful will _____ any budget or list of goals you make. (circle all that apply)

a) outlast
b) outperform
c) depend on
d) be shaped by

Answer: (a) and (b), outlast and outperform. When you know why, how, and what "success" will mean to you, this is your most powerful tool. Your "why" must be bigger than your "how." (P. 209)

Q&A Chapter 10 -You Married Who?

106. A good ______ is your highest-returning good debt.

a) marriage
b) stock portfolio
c) investment counselor
d) degree in underwater basket weaving

Answer: (a) Marriage. A good marriage adds to your life, much like good debt. An ill-conceived marriage, much like bad debt, may drain your emotions daily. Just as your financial statement may be improved, so may your marriage balance sheet. Marriage has a cost in both time and resources. A good marriage creates a dynamic return where the benefits far exceed the costs. (P. 211)

Note from my divorced friend: "Aw, shut up!"

Honey, aren't you going to help me with my bags?

107. True or false: Finances are the number two cause of conflict in marriage.

Answer: False. Finances are the *number one* cause of conflict in marriage, triggering more conflict than issues of personality and kindness. An oft-quoted statistic says that 80 percent of divorces are a direct result of financial difficulties. Selfishness and an unwillingness to defer gratification are at the root of most marital spending problems. And if money already spent is not enough to argue about, just pile on a big old stack of debt! (P. 213)

108. The 19th-century advice quoted in Chapter 10 reads, "Take the daughter of __________."

a) Warren Buffet
b) an oil magnate
c) a good mother
d) a bad father

Answer: (c) A good mother. As I wrote in my journal, "If you do not love your potential mother-in-law, why would you want to marry her offspring?" This doesn't mean that you should have an improper attitude toward your mother- or father-in-law. What it means is that you should seek the attributes you want to find in your fiancé in your potential in-laws. It is very likely that they will be duplicated in your spouse. This advice is especially worthwhile if you intend to have children. (P. 215)

109. What can you do to gain clarity before you meet Mr. or Mrs. Right?

a) Write down what you're looking for in a spouse.
b) Date as many different people as possible.
c) Invest in a dating service.
d) Go to a bar.

Answer: (a) Write down what you're looking for. It's the same thing you should do for every important decision: put it on paper. As we have learned throughout *Good Debt, Bad Debt*, a key way to bridle or restrain dangerous emotions is to contain them on paper. Once you've done that, you have a tangible description of desire. It doesn't sound very romantic, but it worked for me. When I decided that I wanted to get married, I went to my legal pad and wrote out twenty-six attributes I highly desired in a wife. (P. 216)

Darren Hardy in *The Compound Effect* says he wrote out 45 pages detailing his desired spouse down to the texture of her hair and ethnicity. I tip my hat to him. I made a list on a legal pad, and that worked out wonderfully for me.

110. Which of these attributes is not on my sample marriage checklist?

a) religion
b) independence
c) personal wealth
d) delayed gratification

Answer: (c) Personal wealth. When I decided that I wanted to get married, I went to my legal pad and wrote out twenty-six attributes I highly desired in a wife. The amount of money my prospective spouse brought to the marriage was not as important to me as our ability as a couple to plan and delay gratification so that we could create personal wealth together. As mentioned above, the inability to do so is one of the number one stressors on a marriage. (Hanson, 2007 p. 218) (P. 218)

111. True or false: A fixer-upper marriage has just as much potential as a fixer-upper house, car, or business. Love can overcome any faults that may be obvious in the beginning.

Answer: False. If you are the ever-optimistic person who thinks that you can marry someone and change him or her into the perfect mate, don't waste your time. People can change, but only if they want to and their past and their egos don't get in the way. Find the right person first—a structurally sound person. Save the notion of a "fixer-upper" for houses, cars, businesses, and the like. Bad relationships, especially fixer-uppers, bring a lot of baggage and can take years to unpack. (P. 223)

My wife says I never listen to her...or something like that.

112. The "big rocks" idea involves:

a) a landscaper removing boulders from a plot of land
b) a professor filling a container with rocks and gravel
c) the purchase of an engagement ring
d) a cave man learning to play music

Answer: (b) A professor, asked to come up with an illustration about time management, fills a one-gallon beaker with large rocks, then gravel, then sand, then water. Not until the water is poured in is the beaker full. The moral of the illustration is that if you don't get the big rocks in first, you will never get them in.

I call the things on my marriage checklist "the big rocks." These are the foundation of your philosophy, the things that are most important to you. Say your personal philosophy and your spouse's are big rocks. It's best to make sure to have the big rocks in before all the sand and gravel and rain—the daily cares of life—come washing in. Negotiate on the big rocks, and you will probably have a difficult marriage. (P. 224)

Note: I believe this story originated with the late Stephen Covey.

113. Parents' greatest influence on their children comes from their _______.

a) example
b) discipline
c) bank account
d) birthday party budget

Answer: (a) Example. Your children will do as you do more than as you say. Broke and confused parents generally create broke and confused young adults. If parents model good financial habits, however, it is likely that their children will apply them. **"You can't take your children somewhere you aren't going," said John Croyle.** (P. 229)

114. The best gift you can give your children is ______.

a) a strong stock portfolio
b) the ability to learn
c) an inheritance
d) Elmo

Answer: (b) The ability to learn. Learning must start at home. Example has more recruits than reasoning ever will. Broke and confused parents generally create broke and confused young adults. Your children will do as you do more than as you say. When children hear their parents discuss packing Grandma or Grandpa off to the nursing home, the parents are training their children on how to handle them in later years. The same principle applies to finances. (P. 229)

115. True or false: The opportunity to acquire more wealth is worth sacrificing time with one's family over 20 or 30 years.

Answer: False. To gain great wealth and lose your family in the bargain is a poor trade. We have all seen the man or woman who spent all of his or her time on a career while the family grew further and further away. Is any man ever wealthy enough to repurchase his past? No. Not one. Not at any price. (P. 232)

Q&A Chapter 11 - Debt Warfare: When Push Comes to Shove

My wife (Nita's) favorite cartoon:

"Hello, I'm Push, I've come to shove.."

116. True or false: It's best to start debt reduction by paying off smaller bills first.

Answer: True…IF YOU QUIT SPENDING! In my experience, the one with the smallest balance can be eliminated the quickest, freeing up all of its payment to add to the principle of the next bill. This technique was first taught to me by John Avazini in 1979. It is similar to Dave Ramsey's Debt Snowball and several other more recent offers. Ramsey presents and markets it better than anyone I have seen though.

Getting rid of debt really is hand-to-hand, toe-to-toe combat—don't run stand your ground kill the little guys first then use their ammo against the bigger guys. Simple. Imagine confronting each enemy [bill] with your bayonet, gutting the bill, and taking his weapons and ammunition. When you meet the next bigger enemy [bill] you have more weapons and ammunition [cash flow] to overtake the bigger bill. (P. 240)

117. The cost of higher education can be a good debt, but only if ________________.

a) your degree is in law or medicine
b) you can apply your knowledge to robbing banks
c) you get a good interest rate on your student loans
d) what you have learned can be sold in the marketplace for a profit

Answer: (d) Remember, you don't need a psychology degree to wait tables (but perhaps you will feel better about yourself.) A philosophy degree seems to work well for waiters. (P. 243)

118. True or False: Trading in an older car for a new, fuel-efficient model will always save you money in the long run.

Answer: False. With the cost of gasoline so high, many rationalize the need for a fuel-efficient car, and generally this is a good idea. The problem comes from not taking time to accurately count the cost of the new car. The formula for this equation is simple: you can only save the difference. If you decide to trade the old Ford to get a new Honda, what is the actual difference? (P. 245)

Sarcastic barb: If you could save money by spending money, we would refer to politicians as geniuses.

119. While engaging in Debt Warfare, what should you do if you make more money than you planned in the form of a raise, a windfall, or a new job?

a) Hide it under your mattress.
b) Go on vacation. You deserve a break.
c) Stay on plan, pay more, and finish sooner.
d) Invest in a new car that will reflect your higher status.

Answer: (c) Stay on plan, pay more, and finish sooner. Or, if you're happy with your plan, begin a reserve account. In all matters of confronting debt [the past] and savings [the future] you will find that sooner is better, but soonest is best. Don't give yourself a reason to fail at the beginning and quit. (P. 248)

120. The key qualities you need to get out of debt are_______________.

a) luck and optimism
b) perseverance and patience
c) wealthy parents and a trust fund
d) a taste for bon bons and a love of soap operas

Answer: (b) Perseverance and patience. If you are dismayed by taking 20 to 120 months to get out of debt, please remember: the 20 or 120 months will pass regardless of what you do. It's unlikely you got into your present circumstances in a few months. If you don't adopt a completely new way of thinking, you will probably go the other way, getting deeper in debt. (P. 250)

121. True or false: Refinancing your mortgage is an important first step in reducing debt.

Answer: False. Lowering your rate by refinancing may be a good thing, but the goal is to eradicate debt, not to make it a little more comfortable to live with. The comfort afforded by refinancing to lower monthly payments is often short-lived: as relief settles in, some sneak back out and run up the empty credit cards or other lines of credit available because of the refinancing. Without a true change in behavior, you are only digging your financial grave deeper. **That said, depending on the cost of refinancing, and if used properly, it could be a valuable option.** (P. 250)

122. What is the most accurate predictor of an individual's eventual success or failure in becoming debt-free?

a) budgeting style
b) monthly income
c) sex appeal
d) burn rate

Answer: (d) Burn rate. The most accurate predictor of your financial success is your burn rate, or your total monthly spending as a percentage of your income. I like (c) too; sexy people seem to carry debt more gracefully than ugly folks. (P. 250)

123. True or false: Debt consolidation is a good idea as long as the credit counselor you are working with is a registered nonprofit.

Answer: False. There are credible institutions out there, but do some research. Try www.nfcc.org. Just because an institution claims to be nonprofit does not mean it has your best interests at heart. You may be better off following the plan I lay out in the Debt Warfare chapter. If you use the debt warfare plan and are disciplined, you will come out of it having the satisfaction of defeating your bad debt yourself. And you will have learned several valuable lessons. (P. 250)

Negligent Spendicide?: If it were possible to be found guilty of "Negligent Spendicide" the sentencing guidelines would require 2 to 10 years' probation (periodic check-in with your P.O.) and completion of Financial Literacy Basics training, attitude management, communication, and graduating with a mini thesis - a written personal development plan (PDP) for the next ten years. If you truly wish to become financially "well" you need more than a "quick fix" (of credit or income); you need to become "financially fit" and develop lifelong stewardship habits.

- Control Burn Rate, Right Size Spending to Income
- Track and tabulate all spending for the next 90 days (every penny daily)
- Understand tradeoffs, aside money for the future
- Reduce Debt

Negligent Spendicide? Are you kidding?!

Teach your children well...

"I think I'll get a cheaper used car and invest the difference in a Roth IRA."

References

Covey, Stephen R. *The Seven Habits of Highly Effective People: Restoring the Character Ethic*. New York: Simon and Schuster, 1989. Print.

Gardner, Howard, Mihaly Csikszentmihalyi, and William Damon. *Good Work: When Excellence and Ethics Meet*. New York: Basic Books, 2001. Print.

Gladwell, Malcolm. *Outliers: The Story of Success*. New York: Little, Brown and Co., 2008. Print.

Hanson, Jon. *Good Debt, Bad Debt: Knowing the Difference Can Save Your Financial Life*. 2007 ed. New York: Portfolio, 2005. Print.

Hardy, Darren. *The Compound Effect: Multiplying Your Success, One Simple Step at a Time.* New York, NY: Vanguard Press, 2010. Print.

Hoffer, Eric. *The True Believer: Thoughts on the Nature of Mass Movements.* New York: Perennial Library, 1966, 1951. Print.

"Income Statistics." Bureau of Labor Statistics. U.S. Government, n.d. Web. 10 Mar 2014. <http://www.bls.gov/cex/2012/aggregate/quintile.pdf>.

Keller, Gary, and Jay Papasan. *The One Thing: The Surprisingly Simple Truth Behind Extraordinary Results.* Austin, Tex.: Bard Press, 2012. Print.

Linden, David J.. *The Compass of Pleasure: How Our Brains Make Fatty Foods, Orgasm, Exercise, Marijuana, Generosity, Vodka, Learning, and Gambling Feel So Good.* New York: Viking, 2011. Print.

Matthews, William. *Getting On in the World.* Chicago: S.C. Griggs & Co, 1878. Print.

Napier, Jimmy. *Invest In Debt.* Chipley, FL: JimmyNapier.com, 1982. Print.

Payne, Ruby K. *A Framework for Understanding Poverty.* 4th rev. ed. Highlands, Tex.: aha! Process, 2005. Print.

Rumelt, Richard P. *Good Strategy, Bad Strategy: The Difference and Why It Matters.* New York: Crown Business, 2011. Print.

Volek, Jeff, and Stephen D. Phinney. *The Art and Science of Low Carbohydrate Living: An Expert Guide to Making the Life-Saving Benefits of Carbohydrate Restriction Sustainable and Enjoyable.* Lexington, KY: Beyond Obesity, 2011. Print.

Walton, Mark S. *Boundless Potential: Transform Your Brain, Unleash Your Talents, Reinvent Your Work in Midlife and Beyond.* 2012. Reprint. New York: McGraw-Hill, 2012.

After 10 Year Guarantee

Our products are designed for those seeking mastery (not quick cheap temporary fixes) in their personal and financial lives. If you follow our plan for ten years and you do not feel you have greatly profited from Stewardship for Life's program we will refund your full purchase price. I offer this guarantee on the honor system. You must have your receipt; but as to whether you actually cut expenses, right-sized your income to your expenses we will take your one or two page signed letter as proof. We retain the right to use your example or reasons in future writing, or for promotional purposes, *but we will never disclose your identity.*

Simply return the product and send us the receipt showing a date purchased of 10 years prior (address on website) along with a one page explanation of what did not work for you, and why you believe this is true. Include a close estimate of your average income for the ten previous years, so we can calculate where you should be. We do not need tax returns. Just sign and date your letter affirming the income and your statements are true.

See SFLToday.org for our regular return policy for physical products, due to the nature of downloadable products they are not returnable. Thank you.

(Test Only 16 pages) Stewardship for Life's Financial Literacy Basics

You may **download a pdf** of this test and an answer key at **gooddebt.com/test**

Test Questions for (based on *Good Debt, Bad Debt* by Jon Hanson) Use as a pretest or after workbook study and review.

1. Average millionaires, or those on the way to becoming so, save or invest _____ percent of their incomes.

a) 10 to 15
b) 15 to 20
c) 20 to 30
d) 40 to 50

2. According to recent studies, what is most closely linked to wealth accumulation?

a) a large income
b) an inheritance
c) willingness to plan
d) frequent purchase of lottery tickets

3. Which of the following are important steps toward financial success? (circle all that apply)

a) manage emotions
b) work from a plan
c) delay gratification
d) save/invest for your future

4. Who reaps the most benefits from our society's spending culture: consumers or merchants?

5. Those who live in a constant state of ______ become slaves to their own passions.

a) need
b) want
c) hope
d) Nevada

6. True or false: When we use debt to acquire products or services, it's not really a

payment for the product or service, but a claim on future earnings.

7. The insidiousness of debt lies in the fact that the use of debt gives its victims temporary _______.

a) pain
b) pleasure
c) income
d) superhuman powers

8. True or false: In my invisible hand of debt theory, Econowise individuals suffer from the invisible loss of both time and opportunity.

9. Debt takes more from you than just money. Which are among the four major debt effects? (circle all that apply)

a) loss of time
b) loss of freedom
c) loss of cash flow
d) loss of opportunities

10. Most of us unknowingly choose _______ when we subscribe to the idea that "you can have it all."

a) success
b) servitude
c) happiness
d) extra bacon

11. True or false: People who are deeply in debt have essentially spent their time in advance.

12. The first rule of all enterprise is to know a solid value when you see it. The second rule is to be able to _____________.

a) act on an opportunity when it arises
b) calculate an annual percentage rate
c) invest in the right stocks
d) make a grilled cheese sandwich

13. True or false: For most people, massive changes are needed to get out of debt.

14. True or false: Many have a form of wealth but deny its power.

15. The ________ spend all the money they have, while the ________ plan for life's demands.

a) Consumerati/Econowise
b) Econowise/Consumerati
c) Irish/English
d) Romanians/Serbians

16. True or false: Bad debt is debt on assets that create cash flow in excess of the cost of the debt.

17. Which of these statements describes bad debt? (circle all that apply)

a) Absorbs future earnings
b) Decreases your net worth or cash flow
c) Often employed to purchase sexy sports cars
d) Typically used for consumption or rapidly depreciating goods
e) Beats you around the face and head and makes you loathe your very existence

18. What is considered the crack cocaine of the credit industry?

19. True or false: On many loan applications, you must acknowledge whether you have ever filed for bankruptcy.

20. Paradebt is defined as the cumulative effect of ____________.

21. True or false: Owning debt is a way to become wealthy.

22. Good debt is not really "a kind of "debt; it is a (n) ______.

23. A monthly housing cost that does not exceed the cost of renting a suitable dwelling can be considered ________ debt.

a) good
b) bad
c) neutral
d) weird

24. What is the first and most important financial training ground for youth?

a) family

b) preschool
c) college
d) Toys "R" Us

25. Successful advertising generally relies on the customer's _________.

a) income
b) knowledge
c) emotions
d) taste in music

26. True or false: Advertising claims are generally trustworthy, especially when they come from a successful company.

27. Who does advertising work best on?

a) the rich
b) the poor
c) those without a plan
d) those who own at least one margarita maker

28. To become wealthy, you must go through a period of ______.

a) luck
b) debt
c) sacrifice
d) self-indulgence

29. Without control of your emotions and a definite plan, you leave your future to ______.

30. Which of these emotions do advertisers use to win customers? (Circle all that apply)

a) fear
b) greed
c) jealousy
d) the desire to be safe
e) the desire to be loved or accepted

31. Fundamentals are principles that act in a _______ manner independent of your understanding, action, or inaction.

a) consistent
b) profitable
c) damaging
d) geometric

32. The main difference between the Consumerati and the Econowise is their view of what?

a) the future
b) the market
c) other people
d) the TV screen

33. Freedom is found in:

a) a 1967 Corvette convertible
b) a long line of credit
c) home ownership
d) self-discipline

34. True or false: Spending is not a problem as long as all of your existing needs and many desires are being met.

35. What is a burn rate?

a) your fixed cost of existence
b) the rate of interest accumulation on credit card debt
c) how fast you can swipe your debit card at the register
d) the number of miles you have to run to work off a cheeseburger

36. If you are now forty years old, every $100 monthly you burn (spend) knocks out ________ of potential retirement nest egg.

a) $132
b) $1,320
c) $13,200
d) $132,000

37. What percentage of folks at retirement age are partially or totally dependent on government or family?

a) 40%
b) 60%

c) 90%
d) 120%

38. True or false: Regardless of where you're at financially now, you can always make more money.

39. It is your _________, not your income, that will determine your fate.

a) burn rate
b) interest rate
c) college degree
d) movie star looks

40. To "delay gratification" is to:

a) put off a purchase until it fits into your financial plan
b) charge a purchase to a lower-interest-rate credit card
c) avoid your creditors for as long as possible
d) save the kiss for the second date

41. The opposite of delayed gratification is ________.

a) currency
b) immediacy
c) agency
d) idiocy

42. True or false: Excuses can temporarily soothe the awful reality that we are where we are because of our own choices.

43. While both the Consumerati and the Econowise labor and earn money, only the ________ add to the pool of capital available to everyone.

44. True or false: Converting bad debt to a real estate loan can turn it into good debt.

45. You can calculate your reality income by dividing your net worth by the number of _________.

a) dollars you owe
b) credit cards you own
c) years you have worked
d) pizzas you can eat in one sitting

46. ______________ is the death of every wealth-building program.

a) A loss in wages
b) A high credit card interest rate
c) The inability to delay gratification
d) The Democratic Party
e) The Republican Party
f) Any politician

47. In matters of saving and investing, sooner is better but _________.

a) later will work out eventually.
b) tomorrow is okay too.
c) budgeting is hard.
d) even sooner is best.

48. True or false: If your past has many events where lack of money is the central focus, then how you "use" these events as you recall them will affect your philosophy of money.

49. True or false: Your childhood environment affects the kind of life you will lead.

50. It is best to use your past as a ____________.

a) place to live
b) reference library
c) script for your life
d) basis for a tell-all autobiography

51. ________ can hurt you financially from the distraction alone, and is hard on you both mentally and physically.

a) Hopes and dreams
b) Bitterness
c) Self-control
d) New York Style Cheesecake

52. It is important to take __________ of our efforts rather than indulge in pity, envy, and jealousy.

a) a Facebook poll
b) an Instagram photo
c) a realistic inventory

d) an optimistic evaluation

53. The choice we have when faced with life's adversities is always to become ___________.

a) wealthy or healthy
b) strong or strung out
c) better or buttery
d) bitter or better

54. What has the power to pull the past into your present and future, and keep on affecting it? (Other than family, of course.)

55. True or false: Success in retirement comes more from starting and sticking to a plan than from the actual investment.

56. True or false: Our chances for success are better with a complex plan that we sometimes follow than a simple system that we always follow.

57. To apply thrift to your life, you must ________.

a) spend
b) plan
c) have a large income
d) start with some debt

58. If you have debt and low savings, paying a monthly cable TV bill or payments on an expensive car is like paying a voluntary ____.

59. The most difficult part of a plan is usually _____________.

a) the beginning
b) the brainstorming
c) the day-to-day application
d) telling your spouse

60. Most of us fail by ignoring ________.

a) the big things.
b) the small things.
c) the things that go bump in the night.
d) anything plaid.

61. To be successful, we must avoid the great disconnect between ________.

a) knowing and doing
b) doing and watching TV
c) ourselves and our mothers
d) good budgets and bad budgets

62. The more you dislike your job, the more motivation you should have to lower your ______ and increase savings.

a) expectations
b) aspirations
c) burn rate
d) income

63. One quick rule of thumb for determining how much you'll need for retirement is to take the desired amount per year you need to retire in today's dollars and multiply it by ____.

a) 3
b) 10
c) 40
d) 100

64. If you pay $1 a day ($30 a month) into your wealth insurance program from birth to age sixty-five, you will have over _________ if your 65-year average rate of return is 10 percent.

a) $250,000
b) $500,000
c) $1 million
d) $2 million

65. True or false: Writing down your goals is an essential part of the financial journey.

66. Which is more likely to cause us to make poor choices: contentment or discontent? _____________

67. The true cost of a thing is ______________________.

a) the amount on the price tag
b) the amount you pay after haggling with the salesman
c) the amount of life you are willing to give up to pay for it
d) the amount of time you will spend arguing with your spouse about it

68. Disposable income since the 1950s has _____________.

a) increased by half
b) increased nearly threefold
c) decreased nearly threefold
d) decreased by half

69. Retirement wealth is primarily a product of time, accumulation, and _______.

a) luck
b) optimism
c) discipline
d) shuffleboard scores

70. Your eventual success or failure in real estate will hinge on your ability to find and recognize _______.

71. If you want to buy a house, stop talking and start ____.

a) walking
b) writing
c) waiting
d) wiggling

72. True or false: When purchasing real estate, your success rate will be higher if you prearrange your funding for the purchase.

73. What should you do if you lose a deal on a home by making too low of an offer?

a) Call the seller repeatedly with a higher offer until you get a response.
b) Let the seller know that he has lost out on the perfect buyer.
c) Bid higher on the next home.
d) Be polite and move on.

74. If you have an income problem, you can address it through the three Es. What are they?

a) earnings, ear-marking, and econometrics
b) education, efficiency, and emotion
c) education, effort, and enterprise
d) earnings, effort, and entropy

75. True or false: It is generally the condition of the real estate market that determines your chances of making a great profit.

76. What are the three tests to determine if a real estate investment is good debt?

a) value, leverage, and use
b) equity, principal, and income
c) escrow, margin, and depreciation
d) litmus, paternity, and I.Q.

77. True or false: Forced inflation is one key to making money in real estate.

78. True or false: Buying property in an area where major road construction and population shifts occur is a bad idea.

79. When a seller decides to knock 35 percent off the price of a house or other property, he wants to have his money quickly. Many are unable to take advantage of the opportunity because of______.

80. If you are living rent-free (for instance, with your parents) and not saving as much as it would cost to rent a decent place, you are ___________.

a) sixteen
b) foolish
c) too clever by half
d) using the strategy outlined by economist Lei Z. Bumm

81. An easily affordable home is one that ___________________________.

a) will get your children into the best public school
b) will consume 50% or less of your monthly income
c) can be purchased with an adjustable-rate mortgage
d) you can make payments on even if your income is cut in half

82. True or false: The best place to begin in real estate is with a starter home.

83. Generally, as a guideline for lenders, what percentage of your gross income is allowed for housing expenses?

84. True or false: It's wiser to buy a house that's the right size and provide your own storage on-site rather than rent a storage unit.

85. What is it called when a builder or seller allows his bank to collect interest in advance, which is added to the cost of the loan to give you a low payment for the first few years?

86. True or false: Debt for a car is usually good debt.

87. The average car depreciates at roughly $___ per month over three years.

a) $100
b) $175
c) $250
d) $400

88. If you redirect a typical monthly car payment of $383 to a retirement fund for ten years, it could add up to about ________.

a) $30,000
b) $46,000
c) $74,000
d) $110,000

89. If you are in debt or just want to do something smarter with your money, what is the simple solution to transportation?

a) Buy more and drive it less
b) Buy less and drive it longer
c) Buy big and think small
d) Buy big and sell early

90. What is the most popular color of car—and the one that is easiest to resell?

91. True or false: Depreciation impacts us only when we sell.

92. Sales representatives for credit card services commonly tell restaurant owners that patrons will spend up to ___ percent more when they can pay by credit card.

a) 10
b) 20
c) 30
d) 40

93. True or false: If you must finance a car, you should arrange your financing at the

car dealership, where you're more likely to get the best deal.
94. What is the ultimate weapon in negotiating for a car?

a) a large line of credit
b) a good credit score
c) the ability to say no
d) a well-formed spit wad

95. True or false: Cars are commodities to be used, not investments.

96. True or false: Poor record keeping will cost you only time in the long run.

97. True or false: Time spent on record keeping tends to increase your creative ability.

98. True or false: It's cheaper and more accurate to keep records by hand using pencil and paper than to use a software program for the same purpose.

99. Which financial software program is recommended for efficient record-keeping in Chapter 9?

100. True or false: Spending without keeping good records is like flying VFR (visual flight rules) rather than IFR (instrument flight rules).

101. It is best to start record keeping with a _______.

102. _________ is the money you spend but don't really think about, which can add up to a fortune over time.

a) the Latte Factor
b) the Millionaire Factor
c) the Max factor
d) the Human Factor

103. What is a sinking fund?

104. Which tax software program is recommended in Chapter 9?

105. Your core desire to be successful will _____ any budget or list of goals you make. (circle all that apply)

a) outlast
b) outperform
c) depend on

d) be shaped by

106. A good ______ is your highest-returning good debt.

a) marriage
b) stock portfolio
c) investment counselor
d) degree in underwater basket weaving

107. True or false: Finances are the number two cause of conflict in marriage.

108. The 19th-century advice quoted in Chapter 10 reads, "Take the daughter of _________."

a) Warren Buffet
b) an oil magnate
c) a good mother
d) a bad father

109. What can you do to gain clarity before you meet Mr. or Mrs. Right?

a) Write down what you're looking for in a spouse.
b) Date as many different people as possible.
c) Invest in a dating service.
d) Go to a bar.

110. Which of these attributes is not on my sample marriage checklist?

a) religion
b) independence
c) personal wealth
d) delayed gratification

111. True or false: A fixer-upper marriage has just as much potential as a fixer-upper house, car, or business. Love can overcome any faults that may be obvious in the beginning.

112. The "big rocks" idea involves:

a) a landscaper removing boulders from a plot of land
b) a professor filling a container with rocks and gravel
c) the purchase of an engagement ring
d) a cave man learning to play music

113. Parents' greatest influence on their children comes from their _______.

a) example
b) discipline
c) bank account
d) birthday party budget

114. The best gift you can give your children is ______.

a) a strong stock portfolio
b) the ability to learn
c) an inheritance
d) Elmo

115. True or false: The opportunity to acquire more wealth is worth sacrificing time with one's family over 20 or 30 years.

116. True or false: It's best to start debt reduction by paying off smaller bills first.

117. The cost of higher education can be a good debt, but only if ________________.

a) your degree is in law or medicine
b) you can apply your knowledge to robbing banks
c) you get a good interest rate on your student loans
d) what you have learned can be sold in the marketplace for a profit

118. True or False: Trading in an older car for a new, fuel-efficient model will always save you money in the long run.

119. While engaging in Debt Warfare, what should you do if you make more money than you planned in the form of a raise, a windfall, or a new job?

a) Hide it under your mattress.
b) Go on vacation. You deserve a break.
c) Stay on plan, pay more, and finish sooner.
d) Invest in a new car that will reflect your higher status.

120. The key qualities you need to get out of debt are________________.

a) luck and optimism
b) perseverance and patience
c) wealthy parents and a trust fund
d) a taste for bon bons and a love of soap operas

121. True or false: Refinancing your mortgage is an important first step in reducing debt.

122. What is the most accurate predictor of an individual's eventual success or failure in becoming debt-free?

a) budgeting style
b) monthly income
c) sex appeal
d) burn rate

123. True or false: Debt consolidation is a good idea as long as the credit counselor you are working with is a registered nonprofit.

Test Answer Key Only 123 questions
(also available at gooddebt.com/test)

1. b
2. c
3. All of the above
4. Merchants
5. b
6. True
7. Pleasure
8. False
9. All of the above
10. b
11. True
12. a
13. False
14. True
15. a
16. False
17. All of the above
18. Credit cards
19. True
20. c
21. True
22. Outcome
23. The cumulative effect of non-contractual bills
24. a
25. c
26. False
27. c
28. c
29. Chance
30. All of the above
31. a
32. a
33. d
34. False
35. a
36. d
37. c
38. False
39. a
40. a

41. b
42. True
43. Econowise
44. False
45. c
46. c
47. d
48. True
49. True
50. b
51. b
52. c
53. d
54. Debt
55. True
56. False
57. b
58. Tax
59. c
60. b
61. a
62. c
63. c
64. d
65. True
66. Discontent
67. c
68. b
69. c
70. A bargain
71. b
72. True
73. d
74. c
75. False
76. a
77. True
78. False
79. Bad debt
80. b
81. d
82. True
83. b

84. True
85. a
86. False
87. c
88. c
89. b
90. White
91. True
92. d
93. False
94. c
95. True
96. False
97. True
98. False
99. Quicken Home and Business
100. True
101. b
102. a
103. c
104. TurboTax
105. a & b
106. Marriage
107. False
108. c
109. a
110. c
111. False
112. b
113. a
114. b
115. False
116. True
117. d
118. False
119. c
120. b
121. False
122. Burn rate
123. False

www.ingramcontent.com/pod-product-compliance
Lightning Source LLC
Chambersburg PA
CBHW080527030426
42337CB00023B/4653

* 9 7 8 0 6 9 2 0 2 5 2 9 1 *